THE NIGHT BEFORE
CHRISTMAS

THE NIGHT BEFORE
CHRISTMAS

THE CLASSIC EDITION

By Clement C. Moore
Illustrated by Christian Birmingham

Collins

A Division of HarperCollinsPublishers

First published in USA by Courage Books, an imprint of Running Press Book Publishers in 1995
First published in Great Britain by Pavilion Books Ltd in 1995
This edition published in Great Britain by HarperCollins Publishers Ltd in 1997

1 3 5 7 9 10 8 6 4 2

ISBN: 000 198 290 7

Introduction

In 1822, a New York clergyman named Clement Clarke Moore spun together Christmas memories for his children. The poem he wrote featured a red-suited Santa in a reindeer-drawn sleigh, a never-empty sack of toys, and stockings hung expectantly above the fireplace. He called it *A Visit from St. Nicholas*, and it was then published anonymously in a newspaper in Troy, New York. It captured the public's imagination. The poem's opening line—" 'Twas the night before Christmas"—soon replaced the original title.

One reason Moore's poem has endured is that it is a joy to read aloud. Beginning in hushed suspense, the poem builds to a dramatic crescendo as the rollicking verses usher in the mysterious midnight visitor.

A tale of anticipation and wonder, *The Night Before Christmas* has become a holiday tradition in itself for many families. So as you open these pages, whether for a first Christmas or to recall those past, celebrate and share the timeless joys of this enchanting holiday.

'Twas the night before Christmas,

when all through the house

Not a creature was stirring,

not even a mouse;

The stockings were hung

by the chimney with care,

In hopes that St. Nicholas

soon would be there.

The children were nestled

all snug in their beds,

While visions of sugarplums

danced in their heads;

And Mama in her kerchief

and I in my cap,

Had just settled down

for a long winter's nap—

When out on the lawn

there rose such a clatter,

I sprang from my bed

to see what was the matter.

Away to the window

I flew like a flash,

Tore open the shutters

and threw up the sash.

The moon on the breast

of the new-fallen snow,

Gave a lustre of midday

to objects below.

When, what to my wondering eyes

should appear,

But a miniature sleigh

and eight tiny reindeer,

With a little old driver

so lively and quick,

I knew in a moment

it must be St. Nick.

More rapid than eagles

his coursers they came,

And he whistled, and shouted,

and called them by name—

"Now, Dasher! Now, Dancer!

Now, Prancer and Vixen!

On, Comet! On, Cupid!

On, Donder and Blitzen!

To the top of the porch,

to the top of the wall!

Now, dash away! Dash away!

Dash away all!"

As dry leaves before

the wild hurricane fly,

When they meet with an obstacle,

mount to the sky,

So up to the housetop

the coursers they flew,

With sleigh full of toys—

and St. Nicholas too;

And then in a twinkling,

I heard on the roof

The prancing and pawing

of each little hoof.

As I drew in my head

and was turning around,

Down the chimney St. Nicholas

came with a bound.

He was dressed all in fur

from his head to his foot,

And his clothes were all tarnished

with ashes and soot.

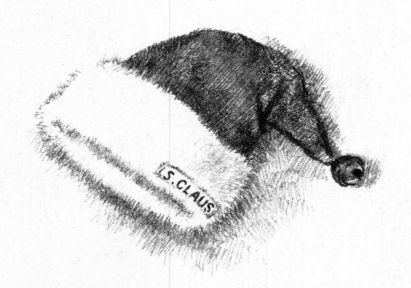

A bundle of toys

 he had flung on his back,

And he looked like a peddler

 just opening his pack.

His eyes how they twinkled!

His dimples how merry!

His cheeks were like roses,

his nose like a cherry!

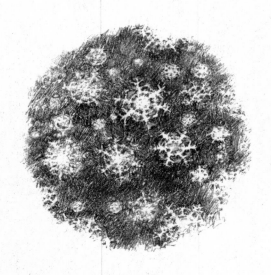

His droll little mouth

was drawn up like a bow,

And the beard on his chin

was as white as the snow!

The stump of a pipe

he held tight in his teeth,

And the smoke it encircled

his head like a wreath.

He had a broad face

and a little round belly

That shook when he laughed

like a bowl full of jelly.

He was chubby and plump—

a right jolly old elf,

And I laughed when I saw him,

in spite of myself.

A wink of his eye

and a twist of his head,

Soon gave me to know

I had nothing to dread.

He spoke not a word,

    but went straight to his work,

And filled all the stockings

    then turned with a jerk,

And laying his finger

aside of his nose,

And giving a nod,

up the chimney he rose.

He sprang to his sleigh,

to his team gave a whistle,

And away they all flew

like the down of a thistle.

But I heard him exclaim

as he drove out of sight,

"Merry Christmas to all

and to all a Good Night!"